First published in Great Britain in 2024
by AYC Press,
an imprint of TELL ME MORE Books

Text copyright ©2024 Shari Black
Layout copyright ©2024 Shari Black
Text effects: TextStudio

ISBN: 9781917200318

WWWW.TELLMEMOREBOOKS.COM

SAY A LITTLE AND DO A LOT

PIRKEI AVOT
(ETHICS OF OUR FATHERS)

DON'T JUDGE YOUR FELLOW UNTIL YOU HAVE STOOD IN HIS PLACE

PIRKEI AVOT
(ETHICS OF OUR FATHERS)

IF I AM NOT
FOR MYSELF,
WHO IS FOR ME?

AND IF I AM
ONLY FOR MYSELF,
WHAT AM I?

PIRKEI AVOT
(ETHICS OF OUR FATHERS)

AND IF NOT NOW, WHEN?

WHO IS WISE?

A PERSON WHO LEARNS FROM EVERYONE

PIRKEI AVOT
(ETHICS OF OUR FATHERS)

BEING CONTENT WITH YOUR LIFE IS LIKE A FEAST WITHOUT END

MISHLEI (PROVERBS)

BUY
TRUTH

AND NEVER SELL IT

MISHLEI
(PROVERBS)

KNOW FROM WHERE YOU CAME, WHERE YOU ARE GOING, AND BEFORE WHOM YOU WILL BE JUDGED

PIRKEI AVOT
(ETHICS OF OUR FATHERS)

BE THE FIRST TO GREET EVERY PERSON

PIRKEI AVOT
(ETHICS OF OUR FATHERS)

WHO IS RICH?

PIRKEI AVOT

(ETHICS OF OUR FATHERS)

ONE WHO IS HAPPY WITH HIS LOT

DON'T WITHOLD GOOD THINGS FROM THOSE WHO DESERVE THEM

MISHLEI
(PROVERBS)

ACCEPT CRITICISM: IT LEADS TO UNDERSTANDING

MISHLEI (PROVERBS)

OVERLOOK FLAWS

WITH
LOVE

MISHLEI
(PROVERBS)

THE DAY YOU WERE BORN WAS THE DAY GOD DECIDED THE WORLD COULD NOT EXIST WITHOUT YOU

RABBI NACHMAN OF BRESLOV

A
LITTLE
BIT OF
LIGHT
DISPELS
A LOT OF
DARKNESS

RABBI MENACHEM MENDEL SCHNEERSON

THE WHOLE WORLD IS A VERY NARROW BRIDGE . . .

JEWISH SONG
(SOURCE UNKNOWN)

AND THE MAIN THING IS NOT TO BE AFRAID AT ALL

THE HIGHEST FORM OF WISDOM IS KINDNESS

TALMUD

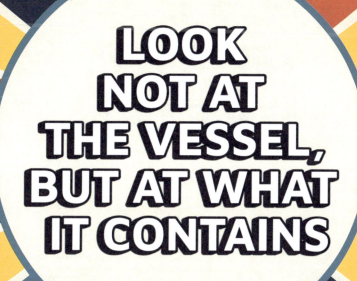

LOOK NOT AT THE VESSEL, BUT AT WHAT IT CONTAINS

PIRKEI AVOT
(ETHICS OF OUR FATHERS)

LET ME FALL
IF I MUST FALL . . .

THE BAAL SHEM TOV

THE ONE
I AM
BECOMING
WILL
CATCH ME

FROM EVERY PERSON

THERE RISES A LIGHT

THE BAAL SHEM TOV

SUCCESS COMES FROM CAREFUL PLANNING

MISHLEI
(PROVERBS)

HUMILITY COMES BEFORE HONOR

MISHLEI
(PROVERBS)

WISDOM IS BETTER THAN GOLD

MISHLEI
(PROVERBS)

UNDERSTANDING IS BETTER THAN SILVER

HEARING GOOD NEWS IS LIKE COLD WATER TO A DRY THROAT

MISHLEI
(PROVERBS)

SPEAK UP FOR THOSE WHO HAVE NO VOICE

MISHLEI
(PROVERBS)

BE BOLD AS A LEOPARD, LIGHT AS AN EAGLE, FLEETING AS A DEER AND MIGHTY AS A LION

PIRKEI AVOT
(ETHICS OF OUR FATHERS)

DON'T REJOICE AT THE DOWNFALL OF YOUR ENEMIES

MISHLEI
(PROVERBS)

JUDGE EVERY PERSON

FAVORABLY

**PIRKEI AVOT
(ETHICS OF OUR FATHERS)**

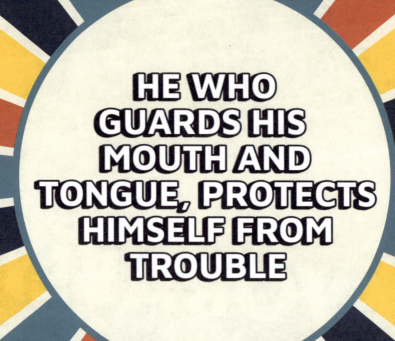

HE WHO GUARDS HIS MOUTH AND TONGUE, PROTECTS HIMSELF FROM TROUBLE

MISHLEI (PROVERBS)

A JOYFUL HEART MAKES FOR GOOD HEALTH

MISHLEI
(PROVERBS)

A RIGHTEOUS PERSON FALLS DOWN SEVEN TIMES

AND GETS UP

MISHLEI
(PROVERBS)

BETTER TO BE RIGHTEOUS AND HAVE LITTLE THAN BE UNJUST AND HAVE A LOT

MISHLEI
(PROVERBS)

PLEASANT WORDS
ARE LIKE HONEYCOMB:
SWEET FOR THE SOUL
AND HEALING
TO THE BODY

MISHLEI
(PROVERBS)

THERE IS PLENTY OF GOLD, AN ABUNDANCE OF JEWELS . . .

MISHLEI
(PROVERBS)

BUT WISE SPEECH IS TRULY PRECIOUS

A FRIEND SHOWS LOVE AT ALL TIMES

MISHLEI
(PROVERBS)

YOUR
WORDS ARE
DEEP WATERS

MISHLEI
(PROVERBS)

WISDOM COMES FROM SEEKING ADVICE

MISHLEI
(PROVERBS)

THE REWARD IS IN PROPORTION TO THE EFFORT

PIRKEI AVOT
(ETHICS OF OUR FATHERS)

BEING KIND IS MORE IMPORTANT THAN BEING RIGHT

THE LUBAVITCHER REBBE

THIS TOO IS FOR THE BEST

TALMUD

FREE YOUR HEART FROM HATRED

VAYIKRA
(LEVITICUS)

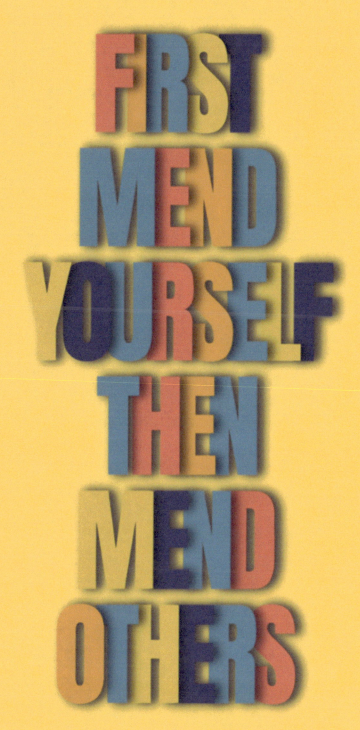

FIRST MEND YOURSELF THEN MEND OTHERS

YIDDISH SAYING

HOPE FOR A MIRACLE

BUT DON'T RELY ON ONE

YIDDISH SAYING

A PERSON CAN ONLY BE LED TO A PLACE THEY ARE WILLING TO GO

TALMUD

SPEAK TO THE EARTH AND IT WILL TEACH YOU

TALMUD

WHETHER YOU DO A LITTLE OR A LOT . . .

TALMUD

DO IT WITH GOOD INTENTIONS

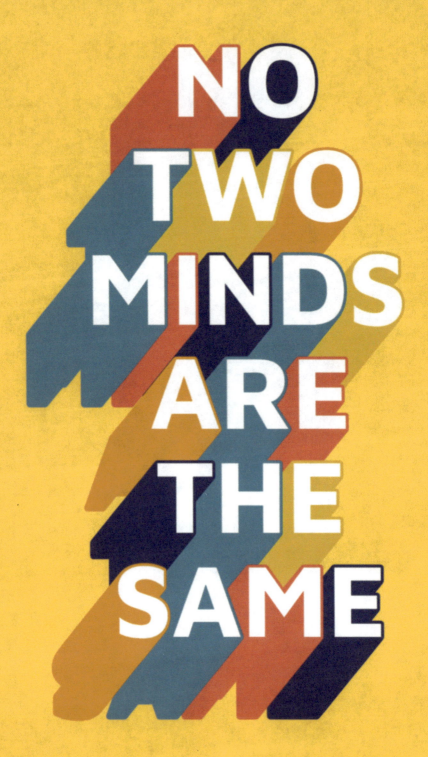

NO TWO MINDS ARE THE SAME

TALMUD

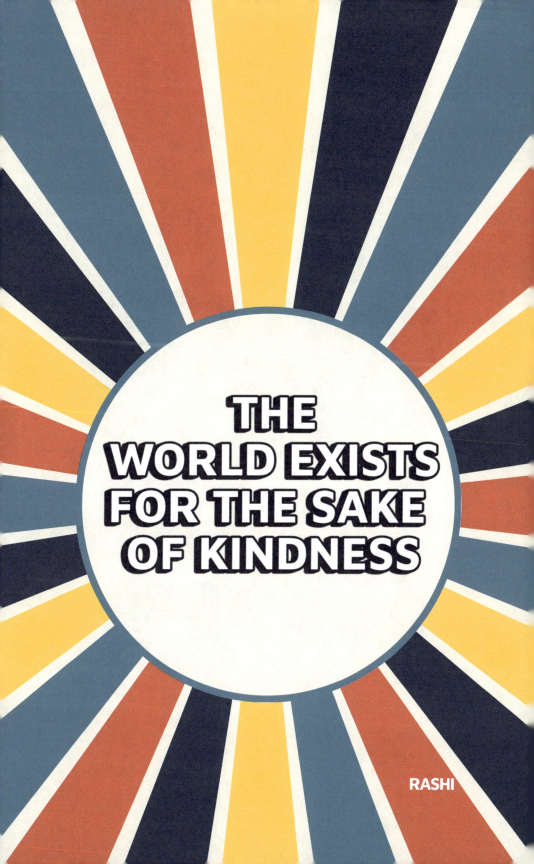

THE WORLD EXISTS FOR THE SAKE OF KINDNESS

RASHI

AND DO GOOD

TEHILLIM
(PSALMS)

LOVE YOUR NEIGHBOR AS YOU LOVE YOURSELF

VAYIKRA (LEVITICUS)

JUSTICE, JUSTICE YOU SHALL PURSUE

DEVARIM (DEUTERONOMY)

THE MORE YOU LEARN THE MORE YOUR HEART ACHES

KOHELET
(ECCLESIASTES)

EVERYTHING THAT WILL HAPPEN HAS ALREADY HAPPENED: THERE IS NOTHING NEW UNDER THE SUN

KOHELET
(ECCLESIASTES)

IF YOU'RE NOT GROWING...

YOU'RE SHRINKING

TALMUD

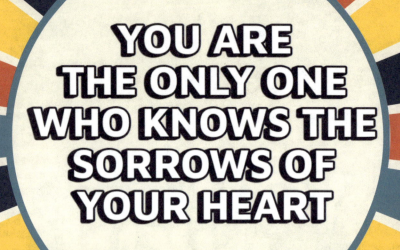

YOU ARE
THE ONLY ONE
WHO KNOWS THE
SORROWS OF
YOUR HEART

MISHLEI
(PROVERBS)

SEEK PEACE AND PURSUE IT

TEHILLIM
(PSALMS)

YOU ARE NOT RESPONSIBLE FOR COMPLETING THE TASK . . .

**PIRKEI AVOT
(ETHICS OF OUR FATHERS)**

BUT YOU SHOULD NOT ABANDON IT EITHER

CHOOSE

DEVARIM
(DEUTERONOMY)

Made in the USA
Columbia, SC
27 December 2025

76973372R00041